5 DYSFUNCTIONS OF A COMPANY

5 Dysfunctions of a Company

Leonard Marsden

Library of Congress Control Number: 2022902256
ISBN: Hardcover   978-1-6698-1013-1
             Softcover   978-1-6698-1012-4
             eBook   978-1-6698-1014-8

Print information available on the last page.

Rev. date: 02/03/2022

To order additional copies of this book, contact:
Xlibris
844-714-8691
www.Xlibris.com
Orders@Xlibris.com
839403

Contents

Dedication vii

Introduction.. ix

Chapter 1   Mission/Values... 1

Chapter 2   Strategy 11

Chapter 3   Leadership.. 23

Chapter 4   Communication 37

Chapter 5   Teamwork... 45

Chapter 6   Situational Awareness Examples 53

DEDICATION

I owe god for everything good and bad in my life. I am a Christian.

I dedicate this book to my four children, Ashley, John, Mindy, and Robert, for giving me purpose to have the drive to accomplish everything I have done to become the most productive man I could be. I also give credit to Michelle, my former wife, for giving me children who have inspired so much drive, purpose, and determination in me since I became a father.

Introduction

I am one of the most fortunate men I know. I had the opportunity to join the army when I was seventeen years old back in 1978. Unfortunately, I got to serve the army under President Carter. We couldn't fight our way out of a paper bag because of Vietnam War battle fatigue, no money, and a weak commander in chief. I was also a part of the military as a young noncommissioned officer, maturing and rising through the ranks during the President Reagan years when we were rebuilding our military. We started training, qualifying with our weapons systems, and fielding great equipment like the M-1 tank and Bradley fighting vehicle and, oh yeah, did we ever start to train, train, and then train again. When I was first introduced to the Second Armored Division in 1982 during the commanding general's welcoming speech, he promised us three things:

1. Good hard training
2. A lot of good hard training
3. By God, if we did not want to be there in the hard training, he would kick us out of the army because people are knocking on the door to get in (remember what the Jimmy Carter years did to our economy).

Hearing the general speak, I thought I died and went to army heaven. And he kept his promise. We trained, trained, trained, and then trained some more. Standards were raised for everybody. If a leader's urinalysis revealed drug use, they were out. It was a great time.

I turned eighteen while serving in Yongsan, Korea. On my eighteenth birthday, I received an $18 paycheck because I had been busted down in rank for arguing with an noncommissioned officer after he threatened me and then later in the day running over a Korean with an M880 truck. It was his fault; I signaled, and while I was turning right, he attempted to pass me on the right; wrong answer. And the final blow to the day was my Korean girlfriend running off with all my belongings. I thought wow, all my friends were back home, getting ready to graduate high school, which I had done one month prior to them, and here I was on probably the most memorable birthday in my life. The only way to go from there was *up*.

Making the army my career, growing and maturing with one of the best organizations in the world, I took for granted things such as mission, values, strategy, training, leadership, communication, and teamwork. That is because it is so ingrained in the culture of the military and I was so steeped in its indoctrination that it became second nature and taken for granted.

Upon retiring from the army as a fresh civilian, I was quickly shocked to find organizations that lacked the basic fundamentals which I long took for granted. It took me some time to diagnose the illnesses of different organizations because like some illnesses, they are buried deep inside of the culture. Some suffered from lacking one or two of the five principles. Unfortunately, I have also encountered companies that lack all five. Man was that fun. It became a problem for me as I stuck around believing I could influence them to improve, and I was wrong. You cannot get a zebra to change its stripes.

I have distilled the dynamics of the basic functions of a company into five major categories, the ones that are the most important functions of an organization and are fundamental to every organization. I have placed them below in order of precedence of importance. In many circumstances, working on one would overlap aligning another area; it is the same with Maslow's hierarchy of needs. It is a sequential list more conceptual for linear thought, movement, and activity than in reality which they are all intermingled.

1. Mission statement and values
2. Strategy, planning, and organization alignment
3. Leadership or how one poisonous leader can ruin a team
4. Communication
5. Teamwork

Where are we? Where are we going? How do we get there? What kind of morals and character will define us, and what kind will we develop and promote? What is our mission? What are our values? Why do we have to have a mission? Why do we have to have values? Doesn't having a mission statement and values constrain how much you can achieve?

Chapter 1

Mission/Values

The shadows of the half-moon faded in and out as partial clouds slowly floated past, allowing only partial light to penetrate the jungle canopy. The jungle's canopy not only blocked most of the external light from penetration but like a greenhouse held in all the smells, moisture, rot, and decay. The heat was hell, and the smells were putrid at times. The jungle was very still at night, with only the usual sounds of nocturnal animals scavenging for food and survival. The soft noise of small animals scurrying around in the night hunting for food and the sound of rustling leaves and sticks hit your senses like shock waves, shocking your heightened senses to peak levels until a fraction of a second after it peaks and you decide that it is no threat. You are hyped up, it is dark, and you are tense. The musky air is thick and humid, making it hard to breath. Your body has adapted to the additional weight from your flak vest, canteens of water, magazine pouches full of ammunition, claymore bandoliers, entrenching tool, smoke, and grenade canisters. The additional weight becomes camouflaged. Then you realize the absurdity of the situation that you are in. You have become acclimated and numbed, simply placing one foot in front of the other without questioning like a robot, a drone, a worker in a slave camp.

Sweat slowly dripped down and oozed from every pour of Private First Class (PFC) Marsden's face, but he dared not move. The discipline to not move a single muscle when you have an itch, need to sneeze, or wipe sweat from your face as it trickles down is a constant struggle and an ongoing discussion in your mind. The consequences are too extreme, so he toughs it out. Any movement, any sound, could give his position away, making him and his team vulnerable. Any sound or movement in the jumgle at night can be detected from miles away by any hunter, and for now, you and the ones you are with are hunters of men. In this situation, while you are hunting them, they are hunting you. You and your team members have developed a sixth sense, making all aware if something is out of place. Any change in the noise of the jungle, the smell, the temperature, or the wind is noticed and mentally analyzed. It is extremely difficult for a squad of soldiers to lie in wait on the jungle floor without detection. The time it took to train this team to develop the discipline, courage, and skill to set up and lie quiet without movement, maintaining full awareness, is immense, but lives depend on it, yours and your team members. After many hours of stillness, the adrenaline rush fades, you are fatigued, but you dare not fall asleep; it could mean death. After hours of this silent pain and constant argument inside of his head, PFC Marsden leaned over to Corporal (P) and ever so quietly whispered, "What are we doing here?" Corporal (P) was immediately angered because PFC Marsden just broke the most important rule: *Don't break silence. Don't ask questions.*

The corporal tried his best to suppress his anger, but it seemed he was always angry, an outburst triggered by the slightest thing. Even on post in garrison, he would constantly walk around and berate, belittle, and show no respect for his men. In return, his soldiers did not respect him. They all talked behind his back. CPL (P) thought he was the top dog and knew all the answers. He was known for pointing at himself and repeating over and over, "We're going to do it my way." Most of his men ignored him and did it the right way because that was how they were trained. They had no choice in the matter and did it his way; they frequently had to do it over. Everyone knew his way was usually improper. He tried to BS his way through every situation and would verbally explode at the audacity of a person for even asking him questions or challenging any of his decisions. His subordinates could see through it and realized he was just an egotistical, insecure man, a bully, who unfortunately, by virtue of his rank, was in charge. They had to listen to him because of his rank. Even though he thought he was smarter and better than them, they knew differently and had to suffer from his behavior because of his rank. If given a choice, they would not willingly give him a glass of water in the desert.

As was typical, in reply to Private Marsden's question, the corporal leaned over and very quietly whispered, "I don't know. Just shut up and do what I say when I say it."

The above scenario is the perfect example of a team not having or knowing what their mission is in an organization that allows a toxic leader to survive. Imagine yourself on the other end of the conversation being spoken to in that manner. Does it motivate you? Does it instill confidence and make you want to work harder? Or does it simply make you want to get out of there as quickly as possible while doing what you have to survive, hoping eventually to move to an organization that is more professional, more organized and properly managed and values its employees.

The scenario describes what it is like not knowing or having a mission. What do you mean you don't know what you are doing here? What is your mission? How does an organization function without a mission?

Whether you are in a military situation or an organization, the mission is your compass. It guides you to where you are going. It gives you direction when you are surrounded by the chaos of the ever-changing environment with the pressure of competition (or the enemy). Most importantly, it tells you where you are not going and what you are not going to do or be. Without a mission, it is impossible to be, know, and do anything efficiently and effectively. The overarching mission should be at a high level but directional, and each subordinate element within the organization should have a clear mission that supports the overall mission.

Imagine any military organization, platoon, squad, or person not knowing their mission or, worse, functioning without one. It would be chaos, soldiers would get killed, and we would lose wars.

Now imagine any civilian company not having a mission statement. What kind of organization would it be? How hard would it be to be an employee in such a company? Would the company run efficiently or effectively? Would it always stay grounded to a moral compass?

I wanted to say this up front, but I decided to insert a ridiculously captivating story to get your attention so that you will read on. If you are still reading, it worked.

Human beings have an innate need to serve a higher purpose. It gives them strength, motivation, direction, and support when in time of needs and questions. Life is chaotic. Imagine life before law, how destructive, chaotic, and violent it would have been. With law came order, a sense of security that everyone seeks and needs. It is one of the first and basic needs of Maslow's hierarchy of needs. Almost everyone craves leadership the same as a child craves the love and discipline of their parents. Children push and test boundaries, but deep down, they know they still need them and are happy they are there.

This is the same with an organization having a mission statement. The mission statement helps us serve a higher purpose; provides a sense of security, direction, and boundaries; and shields us from unorganized chaos.

There are three types of people in the world. The first are the visionaries who see without being shown. The second are those who eventually see from exposure or from being shown. The third are those who cannot see even when it is plainly obvious to even the most casual observer. So with that in mind, keep on reading.

Sometimes the simplest is the most obvious, but sometimes the obvious is invisible to us for one reason or another, and it is not obvious until somebody pulls the blindfold off your eyes. That is when you say to yourself, "Why didn't I see that before?" or this is what they call an aha moment. All I am attempting to do with this book is a simple depiction of what seems obvious with some lighthearted stories that most people can relate to. I want it to be an easy read, and the most important to me is to provide a simple guide of the basics for junior leaders. A junior leader or a coaching manager can take this book and teach his or her future junior leaders the fundamentals of what an organization should always be, know, and do. Sometimes you get so tied up in doing the complicated plays that you have to remind yourself of the basics.

We all know the "big guys" who get paid the big bucks already know this stuff. But they get so busy and so tied up, they forget to teach it to the young soldiers, supervisors, and future company leaders. This book is a simple reminder, guide, and teaching tool.

Believe me when I say this, there are companies out there that are missing the basics, and the stories I tell in this book will provide several examples of that.

Values

What are values?

The stated values of the United States Army are loyalty, duty, respect, selfless service, honor, integrity, and personal courage. These values are a guide for each soldier and how they should conduct themselves in every situation. It serves as an anchor of thought during decision-making processes. It serves leaders in how they should perceive themselves as they grow and how they hold soldiers, themselves, and others accountable. It serves to aid in individual growth, peer growth, and organization growth as they are challenged, faced, and exercised. At times I fail, we fail, the organization fails, to live up to the values, and it is the greatest opportunity to reflect and grow. So they are not only something to live by, but they serve as a tool to grow.

How does this translate into the civilian sector? It translates exactly the same way. It serves as a beacon of how an organization will treat the community, environment, and stakeholders. It also serves as a process for continuous growth within an organization as it strives to continuously improve in business, leadership, and stewardship of all assets, especially the human ones in their area of responsibility. They can serve as the determining factor of a decision when the profits look so handsome but the downsides are too ugly. The values can serve as the go/no-go gauge.

Here are examples of an organization that lacks values and a mission. The company's product line was regulated by the FDA.

Example 1:

Setting: Owner's Office

"We want to inform you that we have hired a quality manager who is FDA certified. And, if the FDA ever comes here to conduct an audit, all he has to do is show them his credentials, and they will walk away. Derrick, we want to introduce you to Len. Len is our general manager of manufacturing."

Fast forward: Derrick (later discovered to be Eric with a criminal record) came on strong and like a bull at about 6'4" and about 250 pounds, wearing a gold shirt, gold pants, and gold shoes (which earned him the nickname of Solid Gold), and acted like a big bully. He would see the slightest thing wrong on a production line such as a drip on the conveyor belt or a crooked label and use it as an excuse to stop the line and make a spectacle of an employee, publicly berating and belittling them. He would actually start yelling over the machines, pointing his finger in the air, stating, "I'm shutting this line down. Shut it down." The line workers were required to listen to him because he was the quality manager, even though the company work rules stated, "Anybody who saw anything wrong on the line was required to notify their supervisor so that it could be addressed immediately." Derrick's (Eric) bizarre outburst would cause all of the seventeen production lines to stop as the employees observed his extreme behavior.

Everybody knew who was authorized to run the shop and the proper procedures. Derrick (Eric) was just a disruption. Within two weeks, the plant manager and several key people from the shop floor left the organization because they could not take his bizarre behavior anymore. By the end of two months of his employment, the entire

Quality Department turned over (quit or were fired), along with several of the shop floor leaders.

After ten months, fortunately, the company had discovered that he was a fraud. His name was not Derrick. It was Eric, and he had a criminal record sheet a mile long. The auditors whom he had brought in as part of his FDA certification scheme were frauds as well. His employment was not only allowed for ten months, but the owners believed he was doing a great job, until they discovered he had a criminal record for robbery, bad checks, and fraud. It turned out that he had not only faked his identity, but he faked the FDA audit, which was performed by one of his unqualified friends.

Because of his level in the organization, many employees feared that his access to their social security numbers and personal information would expose them to theft or worse, and the company ended up paying for identity theft protection for the employees. If the company had any values, the simple value of respect for others would have been enough to cause his termination, but the owners did not hold that as a value. They were only focused on potentially skirting the FDA inspections.

Example 2

Setting: Senior Staff Meeting

"Why do we have to spend so much time and money interviewing people? (Derrick/Eric?) Why don't we just hire people like we used to, who can't get a job anywhere else, so we can make them work whatever hours we need and keep their wages low?" Can you imagine working for a company that values their workforce that way?

"The reason that hiring special needs people is so good is because we never have to give them raises. If we give them raises, they lose their government benefits." This can be interpreted by the outside world as wow, that company hires a lot of special needs people and they really care. When the truth is the opposite; they use them for cheap labor.

"So what if we have not completed our safety training for the year? Are we in business to make money or conduct safety training?" Can you imagine working for a company that values the safety of the labor force so little that it actually not only thinks but also voices the disregard for conducting OSHA-mandated training to prevent accidents in favor of getting the days production out?

These few examples demonstrate a company that has no stated values that allow them to flex their own rules and morality around situations as they see fit. Unfortunately, it never allows them to build an organization with high morals and character.

Summary

So we can see that a mission statement is a statement of how you intend to win in business. It will help a company define and make clear choices on people, investments, and resources, and it prevents them from falling into the common trap of asserting they will be all things to all people all of the time. (1)

The mission statement should balance the possible and the impossible. Here are some examples of what I think are great mission statements. After reading the following mission statements, see if you agree. Determine if you can detect the direction and the limitations of the mission statements, how you could improve them or how you would change them. Compare them to your mission statement.

Starbucks: *To inspire and nurture the human spirit—one person, one cup and one neighborhood at a time*

Walmart: *To save people money so they can live better*

NASA: *To reach for new heights and reveal the unknown so that what we do and learn will benefit all humankind*

Department of Defense: *To provide the military forces needed to deter war and to protect the security of our country*

CHAPTER 2

Strategy

The definition of strategy is a plan of action or policy designed to achieve the company's mission. The military definition of strategy is a set of ideas implemented by military organizations to pursue desired strategical goals. The mission is the end goal; the strategy is how you get there.

Now that we have discussed mission statements and values and how important they are to provide direction, limit actions, and set the tone and character of your organization, we will explore strategy. Strategy is the plan to move toward meeting the objectives or vision of the mission statement. Functioning without a strategy is inefficient and ineffective and can end in catastrophe.

Is it possible to develop a strategy without a mission statement? Yes, but the proverbial "but" is what you would gain and what would you lose by doing so. Here are some examples of functioning without a strategy. At this point, we will focus on what you can lose in terms of utilizing and maximizing all your resources efficiently and effectively.

Senior Staff Meeting

Don't you think we should develop a strategy to align activities and set goals and benchmarks to hold people accountable? Owner (one of three): Our strategy is to make money. That's it, the bottom line, and we are going to do it "my way." Think about what the effect on an organization would be with that kind of attitude. On face value, you would say it is obvious that anybody in business in today's business world would not act like that. The fact of the matter is that many companies do, especially closely held companies. You can look at indeed.com and see company reviews to support this observation.

Back to the meeting: Every person in that senior management meeting received the message loud and clear, the message of just shut up and do what you are told. How is this possible? Why don't people walk out the door?

Answer: Handcuffs. Background and experiential handcuffs—maybe there is something in the person's background or history that would make it difficult to get another position. "Golden handcuffs"—perhaps the person is well paid and can't afford to leave, or has significant debts, or desperately needs the hospitalization insurance. Or the employee's relationship with an owner was so close that he or she will never get fired, even if they are a mediocre employee.

We must ask ourselves: Does this behavior build people? Does it build the organization? Does it diminish people? What could the organization achieve in a more professional environment?

Military Scenario

Corporal "My Way" yelled at his men, "Move, move, move!" The men were exhausted from carrying the additional seventy pounds of equipment while running over ten miles in the desert. The men were physically fit and trained to deal with physically enduring challenges, but human limitations are real, and the environment will extract its toll regardless of the mental agility and toughness of these battle-hardened men. It was about 1400 hours (2:00 p.m.) in the desert. The hottest part of the day in the desert was about 1300–1700 hours (1:00 p.m.–5:00 p.m.), and it was SOP to be conscious of operational constraints and conditions to maximize efficiency and effectivity to accomplish the mission. In the military, success requires a combination of a mission statement, a strategy, training, tactics, communication, leadership, teamwork, and a splash of luck. Anything less is suboptimal and violates the 5P factor, and that is "Prior planning prevents poor performance." In the army, it can mean mission failure and soldier's death.

The canteens of the men had been empty for the last three miles of running in the 104-degree sunbaked desert. The sun constantly beat down on the men, sucking every ounce of water out of their bodies as they ran with their heavy equipment toward a place, goal, and mission known only to Corporal "My Way." They were running out of sweat, and the onset of heat exhaustion was evident. Corporal "My Way" continued screaming deliriously, "Move, move, move!" Ironically, the first to fall from heat exhaustion was Corporal "My Way." As he lay on the ground suffering from heat exhaustion, the men were clueless as to where they were and couldn't call a medevac in to save his life. They only knew that Corporal "My Way" said move out, and they learned a long time ago to not question him or you will be belittled, screamed at, and made to feel worthless. It was best to just suck it up and do the best you could every step of the way no matter where that step would be. Just follow orders and you will keep Corporal "My Way" from screaming at you. They only knew that Corporal "My Way" could die where he lay. Then PFC Marsden took charge and had the men loosen his clothing and provide shade for him. He knew the guy was an idiot, but he did not want him to die, so he did what he could to help save him. Just as importantly, he had to save the rest of the team. He immediately had the men set up security and stop moving to conserve energy and what moisture remained in their bodies. He sent two men to search for a water source. Whatever the mission was, it was now secondary to survival. PFC Marsden quickly devised a plan, communicated it, gave assignments, made sure each person knew the importance of their assignment, and eventually saved Corporal "My Way's" life.

Army normal operating procedures is to receive a "warning order." A warning order is a quick notice to start preparing for a mission; the "operation order" would soon follow. The warning order gave you the operational parameters so that leadership could start developing the strategy, tactics, chain of command, command and control signal, etc. (five-paragraph operation order). After you have received a mission, the next step is to develop a strategy that matches the direction that your mission takes you. Each element in an organization can create strategies to meet their particular piece of responsibility to achieve the mission and strategy. The steps to achieve the strategy are known as the tactics. The tactics can be boiled down to what a single unit has to do to participate. For example, it may be a battle task for a company to survive and operate in a chemically contaminated environment. That is a collective battle task that a unit has to be proficient in to be successful on the battlefield. The specific individual task may be to don a protective mask and protective gear within a certain amount of time. If the individual fails to perform that particular individual task proficiently, they may die and jeopardize others as well. If the unit fails it, it will experience a high casualty rate and fail in its mission. Every soldier has to be proficient in each individual task. Each element such as a squad, platoon, company, battalion, and brigade has to be proficient in its collective tasks cascading through the entire chain of command. The ways to obtain, achieve, maintain, and sustain that level of operational competency require a training strategy.

Each individual is responsible to achieve a level of competence in their tasks required at the rank they hold. The sergeant in charge of the soldiers is responsible to ensure that they are constantly trained and always ready. The platoon sergeant and platoon leader are responsible in ensuring that the platoon collectively is competent in the individual tasks, collective tasks, and battle tasks, etc. And that responsibility increases through the company level, battalion level, brigade level, division, and corps levels to execute our nation's assignments. It is complex yet simple, but you have to do it, and if left undone, at any point, its effect is like dominoes falling to a point of failure.

Civilian Scenario 1

The director of quality who had worked for the company for over six years only worked Tuesday through Thursday. When hired into the company, he was required to develop a quality program. He quickly went to work writing procedures. He was rarely involved with any of the day-to-day challenges. The only thing he did was complain that people were not following the procedures. The procedures filled three full binders, which were only available in the Quality Department. Some were available online, but computer access on the shop floor was minimal, and most employees had not been trained to navigate the computer to access the procedures.

Therefore, the procedures were unknown to the shop floor personnel and primarily served the director when an issue occurred with a customer. His method was to immediately point out that if the "procedure" had been followed, the problem would not have occurred. Then rather than creating a training and deployment strategy, he would retire back to his office and await the next customer issue. When that happened, he would pop his head out of the hole and create a commotion about a procedure that had not been followed again. This provided the owner the baseball bat to demonstrate his wisdom over everybody as he would publicly berate, ridicule, and demean everybody within earshot. Not only the people involved, but everybody in the organization.

There was no strategy to improve. The company was both ignorant of developing a working strategy and complacent based from previous experiences. The quality manager's strategy was "to complain, blame, and threaten" and then disappear after Thursday and return the following Tuesday. Rinse and repeat Tuesday to Thursday, disappear, go home, and come in the following Tuesday. The owners, while disappointed, accepted this as the best that could be done. There was no strategy to improve. They were unaware that "what got you here won't get you there."

Civilian Scenario 2

Sales brought in a big customer order for forty thousand boxes of eight different products, which, by customer specification, would be packed into a carton of eight and shipped. Thus, this was a "bulk order" for three hundred twenty thousand bottles that needed filled, labeled, capped, packaged, and shipped. Typically, for this company, the only planning that took place was the planning the owners were doing when looking forward to cashing the checks. This multimillion-dollar order was, as typical, thrown over the fence from Sales to Purchasing and then onto Operations.

Lack of planning, and even understanding the effect of this huge order on the operation, nearly bankrupted the company. The total amount of product needed to fill the order was very costly and severely impacted cash flows. The size of the order strained the company's supply chain, and some of the usual vendors could not supply the materials in the needed quantities. Purchasing had to find additional vendors, many of whom refused to extend credit to the "new, one-time customer" further straining cash resources.

There was a lot of "in process" product and material cost plus overhead being allocated to the "bulge order," and because the bottling filling machine in the plant could only fill twelve bottles simultaneously, other customer orders could not be filled, further exacerbating the cash flow situation. While new, more capable equipment was needed for this order, delivery and installation would require ten months, long after the customer's due date. Lack of a strategic growth plan jeopardized the company and its relationship to this customer and others.

In addition to the bottle filling constraint, the capping process required tightening the caps by hand as it had always been done. The employees were getting blisters on their hands from the repetitive actions and were exposed to getting carpal tunnel disorder. Someone in the chain of command thought this could be automated and ordered an inexpensive single-head, foot-operated pneumatic cap tightening machine for the line. The single-head machine became a constraint on the line, so a second single-head, foot-operated pneumatic cap tightening machine was ordered and placed on the line to relieve the constraint.

What went wrong? From the start, the owners were blinded

by potential revenue and assumed that it could be done and never questioned their assumption. Of course, almost anything can be done given enough time and money. The supply chain constraints should have been recognized as well as the effect it would have on cash flow. The equipment and labor capacities should have been analyzed and shortfalls and constraints recognized and addressed at the very beginning of the planning process.

It could have been done efficiently and effectively if a strategy and plan were in place guiding the growth of the company. During the planning process, all the constraints and weaknesses should have been brought to the table and each area of concern addressed prior to the execution of the order.

Now that I have gotten deep in the weeds of the cascading issues resulting from not having a strategy, you may have the question at this point of "How do I develop a strategy?" Good question. You don't start developing a strategy until you have done some analysis. An acronym used for one type of that analysis is SWOT. SWOT stands for strengths, weaknesses, opportunities, and threats. Strengths and weaknesses are an internal assessment, while opportunities and threats are external analysis. Let's first focus on the external.

The first assessment that you can do is that of your own industry. What industry are you in? Is it constrained to new entrants by government or environmental regulations? Is it something that is easy for people to get into? Is it highly competitive? Does it take a lot of capital investment to get into? Does it take special equipment, etc.?

The next step is to start looking at your market. How many potential customers are out there in your market? What is your assessment of where you stand against the competition in your market? Does any competitor have an advantage in modes of operation? How long will that competitive advantage last?

Are you known as competitive, a threat? Are other companies keeping an eye on you and trying to gain some of your market share? Do you have a competitive advantage? How long will it last? Are competitors trying to replace or copy your competitive advantage? How much are they spending on research and development as a percentage of sales compared to you? You need a cross-functional group of thinkers in your company to develop any question possible to give you the best common operating picture to lead you to the best decision possible. Stop flying blind in the fog of competition and start clearing it up with some intel and analysis. Know where the challenges are and be honest about them. Don't lie to yourself or ignore them as it could bring about loss and disaster.

You have to know what your competitors ate for breakfast today and what they are planning to eat tomorrow in developing your strategy. If you know where they stand and the direction they are taking, you may be able to create a win-win by going a different direction and fight like a cat in a dog fight. If you are focusing on the status and direction that your competitors are taking, you may be able to think of a competitive advantage that does not directly threaten them and is unique to your particular internal strengths and weaknesses that may place you in blue ocean space as compared to the blood-red competitive shark-infested ocean space.

Example

Gyms, fitness centers, and such. When I was young in the sixties and seventies, the only gyms available was the gym at your school and mostly the YMCA. In the late seventies and early eighties, you could see the fitness fad taking hold, and gyms like Gold's and World Gym became big. Now you have LA Fitness and Planet Fitness, and the environment is rich with competitive gyms, fitness centers, and such. So much so that you can join them for as little as $10 per month. That is a really good deal compared to the health benefit achieved from working out and staying in shape. A person who is a fitness instructor used to be able to take clients or meet clients and train them in practically any gym. Now it is hard because many of the gyms have their own fitness instructors (most I have encountered are not very good or motivational), and it is more for legal and liability issues than fitness. But it is a lot harder for a freelance fitness instructor to make a living like they were able to ten years ago.

I should have listened to my grandpa in 1981 when he told me to start a chicken farm. I thought he was crazy, but look how the consumption of chicken is dovetailed into bodybuilding and the fitness world. As it grew, so did the hunger for chicken. Show me a bodybuilder who does not eat chicken and rice and I will show you someone very unique.

Let's get back to the fitness focus. So we can see the market is saturated, and it is getting less likely that freelance fitness instructors can make a living like they were accustomed to in the past. What can we do that does not entail opening up another gym and just jumping into the shark-infested waters of a red ocean already saturated with cheap but good gyms, fitness centers, and such? What about a tactical gym for these fitness instructors? A gym that can be hitched to the back of their truck with the basic equipment inside, music, mirrors, padding, air-conditioning possibly, and you take the gym to the client. Many self-conscious people do not want to go to gyms and be around other people. Some people need a personal trainer to push them. So why doesn't the personal trainer take the tactical gym to the client? That is an example of a blue ocean idea. While it would not take much to enter that market, you would have the advantage of being first and probably would be able to establish a base of customers to sustain operations. If you were really smart, you would start to sell it as a franchise, gym ready.

So you can see that by analyzing your industry, market, competitors, etc. It can lead you to finding a blue ocean solution. This will lead you to developing a strategy.

Once you have found the space you want to occupy in the field of business, it will lead you to determine your mission as well. Developing your mission will keep you focused and help you develop the strategies you need to accomplish the mission.

Step 1 is to determine the business space you want to occupy, measured against your desires or business direction, and to develop your vision–mission.

Step 2 is to develop the strategy you need to accomplish or work toward your vision–mission.

The most effective thing to do is to make sure you link the mission and strategy throughout your organization so that it is focused on the most important tasks. I have seen time and time again organizations that exert so much time, energy, and resources not directed toward anything that benefits them or toward achieving their strategic goals. I don't know how many times I have seen piles and piles of busy work that may look and sound good but do nothing toward your strategy. It is very important that you develop a culture that is continuously improving, which would include not only constantly assessing your achievements toward your strategy but also determining if what you are doing at every level needs to be fine-tuned or eliminated. It is more important to stop, take the loss, and learn from your mistake rather than being stubborn and continuing to waste, time, energy, and resources.

Okay, okay, I will stop beating the horse to death. It is just a rut that is hard to get out of.

CHAPTER 3

Leadership

So far, we have reviewed the importance and examples of companies or events that lack mission, values, and strategy. Now we are going to discuss leadership. We will look at the effects of the lack of or toxic leadership in a company and the benefits of having a great leader. I am confident that most of the people reading this book have encountered a toxic leader in their lifetime. I have less confidence that you may have had the pleasure of having good to great leadership. As I explained at the beginning of the book, I am a fortunate man. I have had the opportunity to experience great leaders and very bad leaders in the military and the civilian sector (almost equal amounts of time): twenty-two years in the army, three years as a military contractor, and twenty years as a civilian. One thing that always rings true is that leadership matters. In the presence of leadership, you would have a mission statement, values, and strategy, and yet to be discussed are communication and teamwork. Sometimes the great leader is far down the food chain who makes things happen contrary to the poor leadership above him or her. In fact, I have seen such great junior leadership that the executive leadership feels threatened and starts taking steps to eliminate this threat. So the organization may have lower-level leaders who actually keep the organization afloat contrary to ownership or executive level lacking thereof. This implies that in the absence of mission, values, and strategy, it is likely that leadership is missing at the top. This implies that if you are in an organization that does not have a mission statement, values, communication, and teamwork, it surely is missing leadership. Now you see how these things are all starting to align: mission, strategy, leadership, communication, and teamwork. The absence of one of these five principles affect the healthy function of an organization.

One thing is for sure, and that is the military acknowledges the need to recognize, cultivate, and develop leaders. Let me explain. There are very few, if any, organizations that spend as much time and money developing leaders. For example, in the United States Army, at least when I served from 1978 to 2000, when a person became a sergeant, they attended a thirty-day live-in course called Primary Leadership Development Course. I heard they changed it to the Warrior Leader Course and turned a lot of it into correspondence courses (big mistake). I don't know the validity of that, but that is weak. You don't learn as much from a correspondence course as you do when you eat, sleep, and live the lessons, chew the dirt so to speak. But who am I to judge? Only one of the men who lived through the Jimmy Carter broken military, the Ronald Reagan buildup, Bush's certification, and the teardown of Clinton, that's who.

When you get promoted to staff sergeant (SSG), you attend another live-in course called Basic Noncommissioned Officers Course. For me, this was about a ninety-day live-in course. Then again, when you are promoted to sergeant first class (SFC), you attend another course that was about ten weeks in my case, live in, etc. So you see my point. What college or company invests that much time sending people away to live-in courses focused on leadership training? I am confident in saying very few, except for other services like the police departments, federal agents, etc. But we are talking about your average civilian organization.

The impact from the training and graduation is everlasting. You can call it brainwashing, but it has created some of the best leaders in history.

The military definition of leadership is "the process of influencing others to accomplish the mission by providing purpose, direction, and motivation." (2) Purpose is the "why." Direction is the orientation to the task. Motivation is "the will to do everything they are capable of doing to accomplish the mission." (2) There is a significant difference between leadership and management. Leaders lead from the front, communicate, provide vision and resources, mentor, and ultimately care about the people and the mission. An old army saying we had when I served was "Mission first, people always."

Managers manage the resources and assets and mostly care about hitting the numbers, cutting cost, and continuously improving. Some managers are custodians, while others are change agents. The custodians maintain status quo, not necessarily leading. The change agent continuously improves, and that one is the first movement toward leadership. Another thing to keep in mind is I have boiled down two different business models: profit over people and people over profit. I believe good leaders understand that if they apply the people over profit model, people will be motivated and ensure the profit is there with honesty, transparency, communication, and teamwork. What I have experienced in most cases is the profit over people model, in which the leadership team is composed mostly of managers and not leaders, and while they may have developed some financial juggling skills, they lack the understanding that the essence of building a profitable organization is truly focusing on the people. I will say it again, if you focus on the people who are honest and transparent, communicate, and foster teamwork, the team will make sure the profit is there. Why? Because all their hearts and minds will be in the game. And those who aren't, you must get them off the team fast. There is no time to waste on wounded bears in the camp; they drain resources, time being the most important one. You are either on the team or not, in which case you are out. I learned that the hard way. I kept wounded bears (underperformers, backstabbers, underminers, and negative nellies)—you get the drift, people—and they have bitten me in the ass *every single time*, either because of the lack of achievement which could have and should have been accomplished or because of the complete utter failure in performance that could have and should have been done. Achievement is completing a challenging task, and performance is the efficient application of resources to complete a mission or take care of a customer on time and right the first time.

One thing that I have noticed is that most jobs are labeled with "manager." Some examples are plant manager, operations manager, supply chain manager, etc. But with my experience, what they really need is a leader, not a manager. I have yet to see a job advertisement for a leadership position, except for team lead. But leadership is really what most organizations need the most. An organization is lucky if it can find a leader who can manage. Unfortunately, that is not the majority of cases, and one leader makes a difference. And it is not most people's fault that they have never had the training and very few people take the time to mentor and train junior leaders in today's world. You may think why does he care and observe this? The reason it matters is because it sets the psychological state of the onset of the journey. While it may be important to keep an organization as flat as possible, people are motivated by recognition, rank, titles, etc.

One thing about leadership is that you know when you have a good one and you know when you have a bad one. But most of you live with mediocre leaders. You can observe signs of it through the discipline and motivation of the people whom the leader leads.

Example of a very bad leader in the military: "The forgotten soldier"

The Forgotten Soldier

The *whop, whop, whopping* sound of the helicopter blades sliced the night air. The soldiers inside the perimeter knew that the sound meant the enemy was repelling out of those helicopters and a battle would soon ensue. All the soldiers stopped what they were doing and ran to their assigned fighting positions. You could almost feel the tension exuding from the foxholes as the soldiers waited for the enemy to make contact.

Sergeant Gulley was checking on his soldiers and approached the M60 machine-gun position. He knew Specialist Rock, one of his better soldiers, was ready and always itching for a fight. Sergeant Gulley had learned to depend on Specialist Rock to complete all assigned missions with exemplary results. Specialist Rock was a dedicated soldier who loved his country and believed in what he was doing.

"Hey, Rock," whispered Sergeant Gulley. "Yea, Sarge," Specialist Rock whispered intently, keeping his eyes and ears focused on the tree line where the enemy may appear at any moment. He could hear dirt crumble to the floor of the foxhole as the other soldier cowering in the corner moved forward to his M16.

Sergeant Gulley slid down into the foxhole and stood beside Specialist Rock. Rock was peering across the snow-covered clearing, looking for any change in the perimeter the tree line made, with its shadows moving as clouds moved across the sky. Specialist Rock was leaning forward with his hand on the M60 machine gun's pistol grip and his finger resting on the trigger guard. Specialist Rock was nervous but loved this stuff. He knew that he had properly constructed the fighting position to give him solid cover, and he was an expert with every weapon the army had put into his hands. The three clackers with wires leading out to the claymore mines rested on the dirt shelf he had dug out when constructing his temporary home.

Sergeant Gulley whispered so quietly so as not to give the fighting position away to the enemy, "Seen anything?"

"No, Sarge," replied Specialist Rock without looking away from the tree line, listening for the footsteps crunching the newly laid snow.

Sergeant Gulley said, "Rock, keep an ear open for the tool van. That bitch Private First Class Maddox was scared and crying, I had to put her big fat ass in the van."

"Gotcha, Sarge," Rock replied.

"I got to go check on the others. Keep the CP informed on the landline if you see or hear anything, Rock. Later." Gulley climbed out of the machine-gun position and quietly made his way to check on his other soldiers.

Specialist Hollings, who was in the machine-gun position with Specialist Rock, whispered, "Fuckin' bitches aren't worth a shit when the shit hits the fan." Specialist Rock was straining to listen for the enemy and quietly said, "Shhhhh." He couldn't stand Specialist

Hollings because he never pulled his weight and always complained about everything and everybody and was as bad as Private First Class Maddox when shit hit the fan.

A few minutes later, Sergeant Woods, a new sergeant in the platoon, approached the machine-gun position and whispered down, "Hey, Specialist Rock, get the M60 and come with me." Specialist Rock said, "Sarge, I got the main avenue of approach covered." "Shut up and come with me," replied Sergeant Woods. Specialist Rock grabbed his M60 and a can of ammo and said, "Roger that, Sarge."

Sergeant Woods led Specialist Rock through the perimeter; you could see the two dashing, squatted over, crossing the snow-covered field against the falling snow. When they traveled about one hundred meters outside of the perimeter, Sergeant Woods stopped and looked around. Specialist Rock was straining and listening for the enemy, his M60 ready to rock and roll, all his senses were alive, and he had to piss. In his mind, he kept wondering how come every time he closed with the enemy, he had to piss. He wasn't really scared, just excited. He had been excited before many times and never needed to piss. It is just when he closes with the enemy. He remembered one time when he was a private, on an ambush, he almost gave his squad away because he got up to piss. Sergeant Woods broke the silence and said, "Crawl under that evergreen and cover this area. I will be back for you later." "Roger that, Sarge," Specialist Rock said as he slid into the snow up under the evergreen.

Specialist Rock piled all the snow up around him like a fox in a den and then cut one of the overhanging evergreen limbs so that he could see the area Sergeant Woods had told him to cover. Rock then put the limb over the barrel of the M60 to conceal it. He could hear Sergeant Woods crunching the snow as he walked away. Suddenly, he could hear small arms fire coming from the other side of the perimeter. He started playing the scenario out in his mind.

It sounds like they have hit the headquarters platoon. The small arms fire has stopped. It probably was just a probe. They will probably come this way shortly. Why in the hell did Sergeant Woods put me so far away from the perimeter? It doesn't make any sense. Man, it is freezing on this ground. At least I don't have to piss anymore. Ha, that means the enemy must be going around the other side of the perimeter. The army could use me in military intelligence. I could see it now. Hey, I got to piss. The enemy is close. What a joke. Keep focused.

It is freezing out here. It must have been an hour since I heard the small arms fire. My fricken finger and toes are numb. At least I'm out of the wind underneath here. But I am fricken freezing. I need to get up out of here and go back to the perimeter. No, no, I can't. My first general order is "I will guard everything within the limits of my post and quit my post only when properly relieved." Damn it. That is one of the first things you learned as a soldier: Obey your general orders. If I can't master the basics, how am I going to become tough enough to become a sergeant? At least the snow has stopped, and the sky has cleared. I can see pretty good, but man, the temperature has dropped. It appears the enemy has gone, probably because it's so fricken cold out here. Damn, it is freezing on this ground. I need to get up out of here. No, you can't be weak. Now you're being like Hollings and Maddox. If I move, the enemy might hear me. Remember Sergeant First Class Blood slamming you in the head with your own steel pot. Man, that hurt. I only swatted a small bug away from my face. He was pissed because I could have given the ambush away. I need to have discipline and stay put. The platoon sergeant would have a shit fit if I moved the M60 on my own. But man, it is cold out here.

Sergeant Gulley was yelling at Sergeant Woods, "Where the hell is Specialist Rock?" The commander called off the exercise two hours ago and put the perimeter to minimum manning. "I thought he was in the 60 position, but I went out there to relieve him, and nobody was in the 60 position. When I went into the tent, Specialist Hollings told me that he hadn't seen him since you repositioned him before the first battle." The first battle was over five hours ago. "What the %&$% are you doing moving my men, and where the hell is he?"

Sergeant Woods looked at Sergeant Gulley and said, "Oh shit, I forgot about him."

How many times have you encountered this type of leadership in your career? The type of leadership who dictates to you what you are to do and then forgets about you. They don't follow up. They don't support. They just expect results. How do you expect results without recognizing performance barriers to your subordinates? This is a good lesson. It takes time to learn the balance of keeping your finger on the pulse and recognizing barriers or frustrations that your junior leaders are encountering and micro-managing them.

I use a couple of techniques. One is managed by walking around and observing. There is a distinct difference between absent leadership, observant leadership, and overbearing leadership. I have enjoyed the greatest success by walking around and observing and, most importantly, asking inquisitive but not threatening questions. You know what I mean. You can say, "What are you doing?" which can be intimidating. You could say, "I am seeking to understand. Can you explain to me what you are doing and why?" which is less intimidating. The associate will be happy to show you and tell you what is wrong. When the boss is never around, the guard is down. When the boss constantly walks around, people are on their toes more. When the boss stops and shows interest without judgment

(judgment or guidance will follow with a one-on-one with the supervisor in charge of that specific area), their throughput will stay consistently higher than with the absent leader.

Example of a bad leader in the civilian sector

One great experience that I had with an overbearing dictator was very wearing on the entire team. The setting is a bottle filling company that is FDA regulated because of manufacturing over-the-counter drugs. Cameras were throughout the entire plant. I think they had one planted in my office. I would get a phone call from the owner: "Why the $@#% do you have four people on the Terco?" The Terco is a single-or two-head filling machine, and in most cases, it only needs two to three people, depending on the product, size of the bottle, and set speed of the machine. We could run up to seventeen lines at one time. Every time you finished a run, proper cleaning protocols had to be followed. This took time. Also, specific start-up protocols had to be followed, which also took time. So many times, when you finished a run on one line, you floated people to help on another line until another line was set up to redeploy the people too. It is usually a standard two-and-a-half-hour clean-out and another two-hour setup, so the people are floated around until they are needed.

Most of the time, directly after the phone call, the owner would enter the manufacturing plant and start pointing at people, asking them, "Do you know what the &^%* you are doing?" The people were in shock, and sometimes the owner would point to the door and say, "Get the h–– out!" I lost track of how many people I lost because of getting yelled at, belittled, and disrespected by the owner. You have zero recourse, except to leave the company. There is no place to take a complaint to, over the owner's head. All complaints stop with him, and if he is the one making the trouble, it is less likely that he is going to go in the latrine and yell at himself for the bad behavior. He feels justified and powerful because it is his company. You either suck it up and drive on or quit.

As you can imagine after one of those visits to the plant, the production took a significant dive for the day. I would lose people and production. That is an example of the worst leadership that I encountered in my lifetime. I am sure everybody suffers under poor leadership at some point, and it serves as a perfect example of "how not to be."

If you are lucky, you may have encountered a good leader during your career, maybe even with your mother and father while growing up. You can always recognize a good leader because their example stands above the rest. They hold themselves to high standards, set high standards, and help the team achieve high standards. It is not about being perfect; it is about the constant struggle to continuously improve and reflect daily how you could have done something better and catalog how you will handle it the next time.

Everybody is not cut out to be a leader. For one, you must be able to handle conflict. Most people avoid conflict. I have seen leaders who evade conflict at all costs, and it is usually to the detriment of the well-being of the team. It degrades standards and morals, and the leader is just weak and indecisive.

As your career develops, if you are put in a leadership position or if you desire to be promoted into a leadership position, then you need to start a self-awareness and leadership development on your own. Most of you will not have the luxury of being sent to a live-in school that teaches you leadership but will learn more on the fly as you are assigned to different positions. Always observe the leadership around you and determine their strong points and weak points, not for criticism value, but for your own development value. Read autobiographies of great leaders and leadership development books and use the world as your laboratory with the express intent to develop as a leader.

Here is one technique that I have used over the years in the military and outside. Whenever I start a new position in a new organization, I observe my peer leaders and determine who is the best. I find out what they are doing that makes them the best. I adopt their best practices, and I start enhancing them with my own flare, style, and lessons of life and in a short period become the better leader. Don't do it in a bragging, threatening manner. Just do it as a continuous improvement process on yourself, and the performance will speak louder than words.

In my mind, the leader who takes extreme ownership in their area of responsibility sets high standards, works with people to achieve the high standards, decisively gets rid of people who will drag the team down, and sets a tone for winning as a team. The leader is only the conductor who orchestrates each individual's contributions, culminating in teamwork and success.

Some people seek leadership positions because they think they get perks. Here are the unseen sacrifices of a good leader:

It is lonely at the top. You can have no friends. You must be very conscious of perceived favoritism, constantly striving to make sure you are aware of your own biases, treating everybody with respect. Hold everybody accountable to the same level. Don't give some people breaks when you hammer others for breaking rules such as attendance. Don't think that everybody does not know everything that goes on, on the shop floor. They all talk.

You need to be constantly growing and educating yourself in

your industry. Read, take classes, go to seminars, but always stretch your mind.

You need to keep your body physically fit, for the stress that is coupled with leadership takes a physical toll, and to combat that physical toll, you need to stay in shape. You can always find successful executives exercising, running marathons, and doing something that challenges them physically because they know keeping the body in shape is the foundation to keeping their mind in shape to face daily stress and challenges. I recommend working out at lunchtime if you are not able to get up early and work out or if you work too late to go to the gym afterward. Skip a meal and go pound some iron rather than carbs.

In summary, there is a significant difference between leaders and managers, and people are afforded little to no opportunities to be developed as leaders. It is a hit-and-miss world unless you have been lucky enough to have served in the military long enough to be sent to leadership schools or some other institution like law enforcement. So if you would like to be developed in the area of leadership, you are probably going to have to get it done on your own. Success leaves clues. Seek them out from others who have been or are successful. Leadership can make or break an organization.

Chapter 4

Communication

So far, we have reviewed the importance and examples of companies or events that lack mission, values, strategy, and leadership. Now we are going to discuss communication. The army taught me a simple model for communication comprising three components: the sender, the receiver, and the message. Those are the three simple components, but they are not that simple. Have you ever participated in a conversation where you believe you are communicating but later find that there was a complete misunderstanding between the two who thought they were communicating. You were instructing person A to do a task, and they kept saying, "I understand. I got it." The task ended up being a complete flop. We could write volumes about communication, but I think almost every leader and manager would agree that there always seems to be "not enough" communication between leaders, subordinates, and departments. It appears at times that everybody is not on the same page or marching in the same direction which should be to meet goals that lead to meeting the strategy.

For the purpose of this book, I will be focusing on two major aspects of communication within an organization:

- Communicating the strategy
  - Determining the benchmarks for the strategy
  - Determining the tactical steps to meet the benchmarks
  - Aligning the effort and activities cascading throughout the organization to meet the strategic goals
- Determining the score/KPIs
  - Using the score to determine if you are on track or need to adjust and to provide accountability and motivation

As discussed in Chapter 2, strategy is how you obtain or complete your mission. So a senior staff should determine the mission and strategies of an organization, both long term and short term. It does no good if there is no involvement or communication throughout the entire organization. Great ideas are developed by smart people in a room that will be doomed to fail if everybody else is not informed, involved, and on board. Strategy with the proper research may be something that can be hammered out in a short period of time, but that is only the beginning or starting point.

The strategy needs to be rolled out to other senior, mid-level, and lower-level leaders throughout the organization. Then a model is given to those leaders to provoke thought of how each one of them is going to contribute to align with the strategy. The easiest way for me to explain it is to give you a military example, and you can apply it to any industry.

Each military unit is given its mission, and the strategy to complete that mission is developed. To meet the mission, there is what is called Mission Essential Task Listing (METL). The

METL is composed of two different types of tasks, collective and individual tasks. Collective tasks are those done collectively as a unit, such as "survive and operate in a nuclear, biological, and chemical environment." On the other hand, an individual task is required for the collective task to be successful, such as to "don your protective mask and put on your chemical suit within a certain time frame when given the alarm or upon detection." Failure on the part of the individual conducting the individual task would result in failure of the collective task.

Now let's see if we can come up with an understandable example in a typical civilian company. Maybe the collective task is to "reduce the cost of 1.5 percent as a percentage of sales of maintenance costs to 1.25 percent." The director of manufacturing has gotten with the plant manager and maintenance managers and has determined that this is achievable if there is a greater focus on completing preventive maintenance tasks on time. In the past, because of competing priorities, the preventive task completion has slipped to 90 percent completed on time. One of the very experienced maintenance team members retired, and the deployment of a new piece of equipment has drained the Maintenance Department of resources. So it was collectively determined that if a new person is hired to focus on the preventive maintenance program, it could be completed 100 percent of the time and reduce unexpected breakdowns, which in the long run will reduce maintenance costs. The collective task is to reduce the cost. One of the individual tasks to achieve it is to hire a qualified maintenance person or promote somebody within the plant who has the potential and already knows the equipment and could be an immediate force multiplier on day 1 to focus on performing all the preventive maintenance tasks on time.

A person is promoted, he gets to work, and within a month,

the PMs are being done on time, and he has already made some suggestions from his experience with the equipment on how to cut other costs. Win-win for everybody around. Take note that only the strategy and mission came from above. It took the collective experience and ideas to determine the individual tasks to achieve the collective tasks. It takes a team.

I have seen the edicts come down from up above before with zero involvement from the actual people involved with completing them successfully, and it causes resentment, resistance, and in many cases, failure. I have found that if I tell somebody how to do something and what to do, they will show me how it won't work. Have you experienced that? That comes from not taking the time to be inclusive and soliciting team solutions. Being inclusive throughout the organization on the development of tactics to successfully achieve the mission through the strategy is the best means to not only communicate it but also have ownership and teamwork to achieve it. So it is communication through inclusiveness to win.

Now let's say the strategy is set, everybody has been involved, and everybody knows their part. How do we know if we are being successful or not? What's the score? I don't know how many times I have worked for organizations that either had no clue on how to keep the score, never communicated the score, and only beat people up when it was not achieved. How do you feel when you don't know what is going on, or maybe the information is only kept and distributed to the highest level of the organization, or worse yet, the numbers they do keep are not reflective of what is important? Therefore, it is very important to align the benchmarks and measurements to what you really want to achieve and be aware that the measurements will drive behavior, good or bad. So be careful of what you measure. Here are some examples.

Purchase price variance (PPV) is one of those measurements that you should be wary of. For example, I knew a material manager who received a bonus based on the PPV. He was always looking for deals to save the company money. For years, the company purchased sprockets from a local company and had a long-term relationship with the sprocket-making company. The new materials manager outsourced the sprockets to China. Him doing so saved money on the individual cost of the sprockets, but he had to purchase so many at one time, the sprockets had to be stored. This took up valuable, very limited shop floor space to store cases and cases of sprockets. No carrying costs were included in the analysis. There were claps on the backs and "good jobs," and bonuses went out to the appropriate people. Later down the road, guess what happened! The sprockets started failing in the field. The cost of handling warranty and replacement parts went through the roof. No recalls on the bonuses . . . We still had cases and cases stored on the shop floor . . .

I think you get the point. Be careful of what you measure because it could cause the wrong behaviors. Here is another example. A certain engineer in the Engineer Department was measured on the quantity of engineering change requests (ECRs) he completed. There may be a single ECR that is made on one product line for a special order of, say, twenty-five. He would not make one ECR to cover the same twenty-five; he would process that same ECR twenty-five times. What was more amazing is how senior management did not catch on. You get the point.

I visited a Toyota plant in Kentucky and observed a very large real-time scoreboard. It indicated how many cars were to be manufactured that day, what the TAKT time was (which adjusted as orders were added), and if any overtime was required. Each person working in the plant knew exactly what needed to be achieved throughout the day. Have you ever started your day not knowing what you needed to get done that day?

When I was a young soldier stationed at Fort Hood, Texas, I worked in a motor pool. We pulled services on all the equipment. Our sergeant never told us what needed to be done until about 3:00 in the afternoon. That required us to work many late nights on stuff we could have gotten done during the day if we had known. Later, when I became a section chief, each morning before the rest of the team showed up, I would write on butcher paper what needed to get done that day. My team always completed the tasks by 1300 (1:00 p.m.). We had a great brigade commander who was a Vietnam veteran, and he said, "If you are done with your soldiers for the day, let them go." And I did. I also started the day with a formation, inspection, and safety briefing and issued the orders for the day. Civilian companies would think taking that fifteen minutes every day is a waste of time. We never had an injury, and soldiers were motivated and lived the standard through daily inspections. Our unit was in a rapid deployment brigade, which meant we had to always be ready to deploy within a twenty-four-hour time period.

Don't take this chapter on communication as an advocate for meetings. I am a fan of quick stand-up meetings on the shop floor. I was fortunate to work for one company as the plant manager. We held what I called a ballistics meeting twice a day. It had sales, engineers, and supply chain involved in a stand-up meeting on the shop floor. The supervisor would brief the team on where they were at on each scheduled machine and its stages of the build process. Some machines took three days, some took nine days, and if we had something as simple as a waiting on a bolt holding us up, it needed to be remedied quickly. These were machines which sold anywhere from $150,000 to $450,000. This meeting allowed the entire team, from the supply chain to the sales and engineers, to work together with the shop floor team to ensure that we were functioning as a team and helping each other to service our customers. If there was engineer assistance needed, it was immediate, to where prior to me and the meeting, it was when they could come to the shop floor and help us. This really affected the on-time completion of machines, customer satisfaction, and the morale of the team on the shop floor. If they had problems that weren't immediately addressed, they would think, "If they don't care, I don't care."

If it was a part issue identified in the morning ballistics meeting, it allowed the supply chain to work on the problem and provide an answer at the afternoon meeting so that the operations team knew what adjustments needed to be made during the build cycle. And by sales attending the meeting, they were always kept in the loop of every machine and could keep the customer updated in real time so there were no surprises. It worked great. It also allowed the team to develop closer relationships and gave everybody a chance to visit where the rubber meets the road and where all the value-added activities are.

It wasn't ping-pong emails, it wasn't finger-pointing, and it wasn't playing the blame game. It was real, live intel, a situation report, and red flares popped to the supporting team so that we could all be successful by taking care of the customers. This allowed the entire organization to know the score twice per day, especially at the end of the month when the score was really counted by machines being sold and booked.

So in summary of this chapter, like I said previously, volumes could be written on communication, and I wanted to focus on two aspects of communication:

- Communicating the strategy and involving everybody on developing the tactics to follow the strategy. By doing this, you have a greater chance of everybody knowing their part to achieve the goal or mission. This method ensures not only greater success but also greater knowledge and involvement on the direction the company wants to go.
- Knowing the score. What are the important measurements, key performance indicators, (KPIs), or benchmarks you measure that focus behavior in the winning direction?
  - Be careful what you measure.
  - Consistently measure it.
  - Know when to make adjustments to the tactics or the measurements themselves.

By doing this, the strategy will not be lost in the minutes of the meeting notes. If you use this process, it will become part of the DNA of your company and the team-driven goal and performance-oriented culture that you will develop.

CHAPTER 5

Teamwork

Most everybody has watched a sports team execute a perfect play. I especially like double plays in baseball. Most everybody has watched a sports team execute a play very poorly because their timing was off or they were not functioning as a team.

I don't think it is a far stretch to say that most of us have experienced and are aware of both and enjoy the success of a well-executed play performed by a well-disciplined group of people working in concert. I would say from my twenty-five years of military service and twenty years of working in the civilian sector that the military is far greater at teamwork.

Here are some of the reasons I say this. In the military, you have a rank structure, intensive institutional leadership training and great military occupational skills training, and most importantly, great range and field training. At the end of each event that is practiced like response to an air, artillery, and ground attack, the leadership is not only performing the collective tasks and observing the individual tasks but also determining the strengths and weaknesses so that we can retrain and conduct the drill over and over until we meet the standard. It is demanding, and they have total control, but everybody is focused and improves. After each event, we conducted an after-action review (AAR), pointing out what we did well and those things we need to improve. Each person on the team walked away knowing what we had to focus on until it became instinct. The same in sports, the individual works hard, and the team practices, practices, and practices until they get it right.

It is a little harder in the civilian sector because most of the time you only get one chance at the play. Did you make it right the first time and ship when promised? Failure means rework, added cost, and customer disappointment. To many, "it's just a job," and they go home not caring. To a few, they take it personal and dig in deep to perform better.

Another reality is that the military has a rank structure and defined jobs. You have to be recommended to go to promotion boards, and it is how well you performed on the promotion board, along with a slew of other activities you are measured on such as your physical test (PT) score. The higher your score, the more promotion points you get. How much schooling, including correspondence courses, you have taken on your own time gives you more promotion points. In short, it is how determined and disciplined you are in several areas which determines if you get promoted. As opposed to the real world, you cannot stab people in the back to get promoted.

Here is a personal story: When I retired from the army, I was hired as a supervisor on the shop floor. I went in just like another assignment and started doing what I have been trained to do: improve the operation, focus on safety, and develop the team. The difference started showing up in a short time. Our area was safer, cleaner, and performing better than the rest of the departments led by civilian supervisors. There were five of us in total. Unbeknownst to me, this caused resentment, and they were undermining me behind my back. Luckily, the senior leaders were just interested in performance, and while they stayed supervisors within two years, I had my own plant. This is a perfect example of most conditions of people giving lip service to teamwork but really functioning in their own interest, stabbing you in the back.

One technique I use when moving either within a company or to another company is that I observe the best performer and understand what makes them the best. Then I use their formula for success and add my determination, discipline, and bulldog, relentless, "don't quit" attitude and quickly become the best. Are you as good as the best? Do you set personal goals to do better? I can tell you that in most cases, it was not me; it was the team. I only provided leadership and coaching, set standards and high benchmarks, celebrate success, and reward the team. That motivated them to win, which is an indication of teamwork.

Civilian example of poor teamwork

The end of the month is just hours away. The operations team needs to not only finish the machine that will add $450,000 to the monthly financial statements but also complete all the quality test runs and necessary adjustments. The team consists of an electrician, who also doubles as the crane operator and experienced loader to drive the piece of equipment on the flatbed when it is completed. Other members include the plant manager, the quality associate who will conduct all the test runs and pre-shipping quality checks, a shop floor supervisor, and two equipment builders. The clock is ticking; the flatbed must be loaded and must pass through the gate prior to midnight. The accounting team is in the front office waiting for operations to complete the machine so they can start the month-end closing process.

The reason the machine was not completed in a timelier manner is because the operations team was waiting for the part coming from China. The container holding the part was held up and lost by customs at the port. The supply chain had been tracking it, and it finally arrived on the final day of the month. The president of the company expressed to the plant manager that the company needed that machine to get loaded and cross the gate by midnight. The plant manager rallied the team, and the team went into full build mode. It is amazing how a crisis can motivate a team and the fluidity of how well it can work together to achieve the common goal.

It was 11:30 p.m. when the machine was driven onto the flatbed of the truck and 11: 50 when it drove out of the gate, and now it was the turn of the accounting team to do its thing. The plant manager texted the president minutes before midnight with a simple message, "Touchdown, sir."

You might be thinking this is an example of teamwork, and it was on the operations team. Why? Because they cared and had pride and the plant manager was working alongside them, motivating them to complete the mission.

Why is it an example of poor teamwork? Because I am not only talking about small-team teamwork. I am talking about organizational teamwork. The supply chain/purchasing department did not have skin in the game. They were informed all month long of the parts shortages and showed no sense of urgency. While we were working until midnight, where were they? They were snug in bed with no concern if the machine was shipped or not. That is not teamwork.

Military example of poor teamwork

I don't have any. Maybe it was all the years of training beside some of the greatest Americans alive or the fact that we didn't go home until we got it right. We had that luxury, and everybody knew what they had to do. We won as a team, and we lost as a team. Each leader and soldier felt the impact, and we had pride.

So far, we have reviewed the importance and examples of companies or events that lack mission, values, strategy, leadership, and two key elements of communication. Now we are going to discuss the final element of what I call the five dysfunctions of a company, and that is teamwork.

I would not be going too far out on a limb to say that for any champion team, be it in sports, military, or the civilian sector, when all five elements are clicking, it is all coupled together with a single-minded laser focus that results in winning wars, World Series, Super Bowls, the next big contract or projects for a company, and its ability to support and take care of the team members' families, and the lineage of success goes on however you can imagine it. Success leaves clues.

The mission was to take and secure a bridge. Imagine this: The artillery shells landed on a village, not near the bridge. The airborne infantry was dropped in a town twenty miles away, and the bridge had no relevance to the upcoming mission. It would be a total waste of time and resources and could possibly lead to death. Why? Because they were not coordinated to work as a team to meet the objective.

I have seen this time and time again in the civilian sector where divisions are working in silos and their efforts work against one another. The sales team just takes orders and makes promises that production is unable to keep because of an already-big backlog. The supply chain buys stuff that they can get cheap, and there is no place to put the stuff. Operations is just left to deal with it. The supply chain also did not order what is needed for production to build it on time, and production did not staff up enough to complete the mission. The opportunity is there to make more money, but because they are not functioning as a team, they actually are costing more money.

The customers are mad because they didn't get what they ordered on time. But the sales team got their bonuses for exceeding the sales goal. The supply chain is celebrating because they purchased stuff on the cheap and saved a lot of money, and the big boss got his PPV bonus and bought cake. The production team is frustrated because they have been working overtime all spring and summer, building stuff, only to find out that in the middle of it, they are missing critical components and have an unsafe work environment because of the abundance of material that is not needed for six months in the aisles and on the floor and simply put all over the place because they were told to "find a spot, make it happen."

The good news is that teamwork is probably the easiest of all the five dysfunctions to fix. And if you have gotten to this point in the book and apply all previous chapters, you will have teamwork.

1. A mission statement and values
2. Strategy, planning, and organizational alignment
3. Leadership
4. Communication

You will have teamwork if you have all of the above. Here are some suggestions on developing teamwork at different levels.

Senior staff must get out of the office and develop deep relationships. They need to see each other not only as colleagues but also as people and friends whom they would bend over backward for. Because if they develop this relationship, they will work together, not against each other, and the alignment of activities start at the top.

Mid-level managers need to do the same. Senior staff need to develop relationships aligned not only with their own areas of responsibility but also with all other functional managers. Success will depend on relationships. When your desire to win as an organization is based on the essence of not wanting to let your other team members down, versus selfish reasons, you have found the secret essence.

Each person, from the CEO to the janitor, needs to see themselves as servants to all. They are all equal, with different parts to play to achieve those touchdowns, home runs, and double plays, get that next order; you get the picture. They just have different functions on the team. The CEO could not function without the janitor, and the janitor could not function without the CEO. If everybody sees themselves as a servant to others within the organization and not greater, or better, but as equals with a single goal in mind, then the organization will function as a team.

Like in the beginning, I started out with "I am a lucky man. I have had the opportunities to work with the worst and the mediocre, and I have finally found the best, a company with a mission, vision, strategy, leadership, communication, and teamwork. HUA – it means heard, understand, and acknowledged. Whoa!

CHAPTER 6

Situational Awareness Examples

Superman Syndrome

I included this chapter because I wanted to point out some situations that I know you have encountered but may not be able to pinpoint or know how to deal with. Here are a few examples of environments that you need to be aware of and the signs and underlying issues.

The first is the Superman scenario. I worked in a place where it would seem like little bonehead things were always happening to stop production. That bin of parts that you knew you cut, drilled, and delivered came up missing. Some little things that could stop production always occurred, and it seemed like it was the same person who would solve the issue for you. Ta-da, the Superman cape to save the day.

But in reality, the person was creating the condition to save the day and be the hero. Some people do this out of a survival instinct driven by the lack of knowledge or insecurity. They feel insecure in their position, or they have some kind of substance abuse problem which drives their paranoid, insecure behavior. They create an emergency, watch everybody run around in emergency expedite mode, and seem to pull the rabbit out of the hat just in the nick of time. Sometimes in a union environment, if you do not have visual systems and strong supervision, the union members can create these conditions to create an overtime situation. When you have supervision that grew from the union, they are usually complacent in facilitating that overtime condition. I worked in one company which I found out later that so many people were related to each other that it was impossible to distinguish the nonunion members who were covertly acting for the union members because they were related. My remedy is to fire them.

Territorial Homegrowns

The next environment is somewhat an extension of the first. An organization that grows from $15 million to $200 million experiences a shift in organizational structure. In many cases, as the organization grows, it grows organically, filling the new higher-level positions with that person who used to sweep the manufacturing shop floor. I have seen this, and it was merited. A person who started sweeping the floor, who eventually achieved their BS in accounting, an MBA, and a CPA became an accountant, then a senior accountant, a controller, and eventually the vice president. That is a perfect example of organic growth when a person moves up the food chain but fails to support it with hard work and credentials.

The environment that I am going to talk about is the one where people are moved up the food chain organically but never go to school and support it with credentials. They become territorial and protective. Their experiences are limited to the place where they were promoted, and when there are others who are not organic to the organization with the credentials and experience, they become insecure and territorial and start working against organizational improvements. They will nod their heads north and south in meetings and say, "That's a great idea," but behind the scenes, they know where all the hidden buttons and strings are to subvert the efforts so that they can maintain control. In some circumstances, they can deploy the Superman Syndrome, but the smart ones do it, and you never know. They are primitive survivors, with themselves at the forefront of effort. If they were to ever lose their position in that company, it would be hard for them to make the same money somewhere else because they failed to exert the effort to support their position with credentials. My remedy is to support, encourage, and make it a condition of employment to seek credentials. It doesn't need to happen overnight, but continuous improvement is the keyword until they feel confident and secure enough to let go of the control and work as a team for the betterment of the organization.

Conclusion

In the previous chapters, I gave the five dysfunctions I see in an organization. I have tried to apply experience, examples, humor, and food for thought. Some will read it, and it will provoke thought. They will add to it but see it as the pillars necessary to develop an efficient and effective organization. Most companies work, make money, and survive without awareness or caring about these five areas. But how much better could they be? How much more money could they make? How many lives could they positively impact? It is a subjective assessment, but come on, you know it's true.

I hope you found the book an easy read, found some insights, and had a little laugh. Thank you for purchasing it and reading it.

Bulldog 7 out!

References:

1. Jack Welch and Suzy Welch, *Winning* (HarperCollins, 2005).
2. 2. *Field Manual 22-100, Military Leadership, July 31, 1990* (IL Holdridge, 1999).

www.ingramcontent.com/pod-product-compliance
Lightning Source LLC
Chambersburg PA
CBHW031157250726
48655CB00002B/1003